CW00822742

DRESDEN
Barock

MUSICAL SIGHTSEEING
MUSIKALISCHE STADTANSICHTEN

ISBN 3-937406-41-7

Editorial Direction / Lori Münz
Art Direction and Design / Michael Holfelder / studio holfelder
Foreword and Text / Kristina Faust

EarBooks is a division of edel CLASSICS GmbH
For more information about EarBooks please visit www.earbooks.net

Produced by optimal media production GmbH Röbel / Germany
Printed and manufactured in Germany

VORWORT

Dresden – Elbflorenz – Stein gewordene Musik!

»Die Stadt Dresden scheinet gleichsam nur ein bloßes
Lustgebäude zu seyen, worinnen sich alle Erfindungen
der Baukünste angenehm miteinander vermischen, und
doch besonders betrachten lassen.
Ein Fremder hat fast ein paar Monathe damit
zuzubringen, wenn er alles, was dieser Ort schönes und
prächtiges hat, in Augenschein nehmen will.«
Johann Michael von Loen, 1718

Die sächsischen Fürsten liebten den großen Auftritt
und schufen sich die Bühne für das prunkvolle
Hofleben. Dem barocken Ideal entsprechend sollten
sich die einzelnen Künste im Gesamtkunstwerk
vereinen. Neben hervorragenden Baumeistern und
Bildhauern zog der Kunstsinn der Herrscher auch
namhafte Maler an, denen die Panoramen der Stadt,
das Leben des Hofes und der Einwohner lohnende
Motive boten.

Einige der schönsten Bilder des Barock versammelt
dieses Buch, die Ahnung früherer Blüte zu erwecken.
Insbesondere die Gemälde des Venezianers
Bernardo Bellotto, der von seinem künstlerischen
Vorbild und Onkel den Beinamen „Canaletto"
übernahm, hinterlassen einen lebendigen Eindruck
der sächsischen Residenz um die Mitte des 18.
Jahrhunderts. Szenische Stiche und Illustrationen
runden das historische Bild der Stadt ab.

FOREWORD

Dresden—Florence on the Elbe—Music in Stone

»The city of Dresden does seem a singular structure of delight. All inventions in architecture are pleasantly melded, but allow for an exquisite view. It might take a stranger months to get a glimpse of all of the beautiful and magnificent things the location has to offer.«
Johann Michael von Loen, 1718

Saxony's sovereigns loved pomp and circumstance and they created a stage for the theater of royal life. In keeping with Baroque ideals, all forms of art were meant to be joined to create a Gesamtkunstwerk. The cultural flair of the ruling class not only attracted architects and sculptors, but the greatest painters of era as well. The city's panoramas, courtly affairs, and citizens provided rewarding motifs for artists.

Some of the most beautiful Baroque paintings have been assembled in this book—a taste of the cultural blossoming of yesteryear. Works by the Venetian painter, Bernardo Bellotto, who borrowed the name "Canaletto" from his uncle and painterly role model, bring to life impressions of Saxony's electoral residence at the middle of the 18th century. Scenic engravings and illustrations round out the historic picture of the city.

EINE REISE
INS BAROCKE DRESDEN

Bernardo Bellottos Ansichten Dresdens sind
wunderbar geeignet, die barocke Residenzstadt vor dem
geistigen Auge neu erstehen zu lassen.

Er stellt uns einen breiten Ausschnitt seiner Bewohner dar
und gruppiert sie auf Plätzen und Straßen zur lebendigen
Staffage der photographisch exakten Ölgemälde.

Anhand der kleinen nebenstehenden Karte lassen sich
die Standpunkte, die der Künstler für seine Aufnahmen
wählte, recht genau nachvollziehen und auch im modernen
Stadtbild wiederfinden.

❦ ❦ ❦

TRAVELING TO
BAROQUE PERIOD DRESDEN

Bernardo Belloto's panoramic paintings of Dresden are
the perfect means to form a mental image of the electoral
residence during the baroque era.

He depicts a cross-section of the citizenry, placing figures
on streets and squares as if he were decorating his exact,
photorealistic oil paintings with life.

Following the map on the right it is possible to pinpoint the
locations from which the artist viewed his motifs—and to
find these places in modern Dresden.

1
DIE EHEMALIGEN
FESTUNGSWERKE IN DRESDEN
(THE FORMER WALL
FORTIFICATIONS OF DRESDEN)
1748–1751, 132 x 236 cm
p. 96–99

2
DER ZWINGERGRABEN IN DRESDEN
(THE ZWINGERGRABEN IN DRESDEN)
1749–1753, 133 x 235 cm
p. 92–95

3
DER ZWINGERHOF IN DRESDEN
(THE ZWINGERHOF IN DRESDEN)
1749–1753, 132 x 236 cm
p. 88–91

4
DRESDEN VOM LINKEN ELBUFER
UNTERHALB DER FESTUNGSWERKE
(DRESDEN FROM THE L. BANK OF THE
ELBE, BELOW THE OLD CITY WALL)
1748, 135 x 238 cm
p. 16–21

5
DER ALTMARKT IN DRESDEN VON
DER SCHLOSSGASSE AUS
(THE ALTMARKT IN DRESDEN
AS SEEN FROM SCHLOSSGASSE)
1751, 137 x 238 cm
p. 60–63

13
DRESDEN VOM RECHTEN
ELBUFER UNTERHALB DER
AUGUSTUSBRÜCKE (DRESDEN
FROM THE LEFT BANK OF THE ELBE
BELOW THE AUGUSTUS BRIDGE)
1748, 133 x 237 cm, p. 22–27

6
DER ALTMARKT IN DRESDEN VON
DER SEEGASSE AUS
(THE ALTMARKT IN DRESDEN
AS SEEN FROM SEEGASSE)
1751, 137 x 239 cm
p. 64–69

14
DER NEUSTÄDTERMARKT
IN DRESDEN
(NEUSTÄDTERMARKT IN DRESDEN)
1750/51, 134 x 236 cm
p. 84–87

8/7
DIE FRAUENKIRCHE IN DRESDEN
1751–1753, 193 x 186 cm, p. 78–80;
DIE EHEMALIGE KREUZKIRCHE
IN DRESDEN (THE FORMER
KREUZKIRCHE IN DRESDEN)
1751–1753, 196 x 186 cm, p. 81

15
DRESDEN VOM RECHTEN ELBUFER
OBERHALB DER AUGUSTUSBRÜCKE
(DRESDEN FROM THE LEFT
BANK OF THE ELBE ABOVE
THE AUGUSTUS BRIDGE)
1747, 132 x 236 cm, p. 32–37

9
DIE TRÜMMER DER EHEMALIGEN
KREUZKIRCHE IN DRESDEN
(THE RUINS OF THE FORMER
KREUZKIRCHE IN DRESDEN)
1765, 80 x 110 cm
p. 82–83

10
DRESDEN VOM LINKEN ELBUFER
OBERHALB DES ALTSTÄDTER
BRÜCKENKOPFES (DRESDEN
AS SEEN FROM THE LEFT BANK
OF THE ELBE ABOVE THE
ALTSTÄDTER BRIDGE HEAD)
1748, 133 x 235 cm, p. 28–31

11
DER NEUMARKT IN DRESDEN
VON DER MORITZSTRASSE AUS
(NEUMARKT IN DRESDEN AS
SEEN FROM MORITZSTRASSE)
1749–1751, 135 x 237 cm
p. 70–71

12
DER NEUMARKT IN DRESDEN
VOM JÜDENHOFE AUS
(NEUMARKT IN DRESDEN AS
SEEN FROM THE JÜDENHOFE)
1749–1751, 136 x 237 cm
p. 72–77

DIE STADT
UND DAS LAND

Im 18. Jahrhundert war die europäische Stadt
noch streng von ihrem Umland abgegrenzt
und die nähere Umgebung noch ausgesprochen
ländlich. Umso erstaunlicher wirkten die gebauten
„Wunder", welche die Städte in ihren Mauern
versammelten.

Schon aus der Ferne kündeten Kuppeln und
Türme vom Anspruch und dem Ruhme ihrer
Herrscher und Bewohner.

THE CITY AND
THE COUNTRYSIDE

During the 18th century European cities were
strictly separated from the countryside surrounding
them. The landscape was profoundly rural. Thus
the wonderful buildings within the city's boundries
were all the more astounding.

Visible at great distances, the turrets and towers
announced the fame and pretense of the city's rulers
and inhabitants to anyone approaching.

BERNARDO. BELLOTO
DETTO. CANALETTO
F. ANNO. 17.. IN DRESD

BERNARDO BELLOTO
DETTO CANALETO

AUF DEM WEG
ZU BAROCKER BLÜTE

Seit 1547 war Dresden die Hauptstadt des Kurfürstentums Sachsen und erlangte
zunehmend Bedeutung. Rund um das Schloss entstanden nun bedeutende Bauwerke.
Doch erst gegen Ende des 17. Jahrhunderts begann das Bauprogramm, das maßgeblich
von August dem Starken und seinem Sohn vorangetrieben wurde.
In die Geschichte eingegangen ist diese Zeit als Augusteisches Zeitalter.

König und Adel schufen sich die Bühne für glanzvolle, verschwenderische
Hofhaltung, für Feste und Vergnügen. Doch auch die Bürger der Stadt bewiesen mit
dem Bau der Frauenkirche, dass sie den Künsten nicht abgeneigt waren.

Die Entwicklung von der spätmittelalterlich geprägten Stadt hin zu barocker
Festkultur wird auf den folgenden Stichen und Gemälden nachgezeichnet.

❧ ❧ ❧

BAROQUE COMES INTO FULL BLOOM

After 1547 Dresden became the capital of the sovereign electorate, Saxony. The
city became increasingly important for the region. Near the palace, a number of
distinguished buildings were erected. But the real building boom didn't begin until
the end of the 17th century when August „the strong" and his son came to power.
The Augusteisches era began.

The king and noble classes created a stage for brilliant, extravagant, courtly
ceremonies, for celebrations, and for their own amusement. The commoners proved
their taste for art and culture by constructing the Frauenkirche.
Dresden's evolution from medieval city structures to celebratory Baroque culture is
documented in the following paintings and engravings.

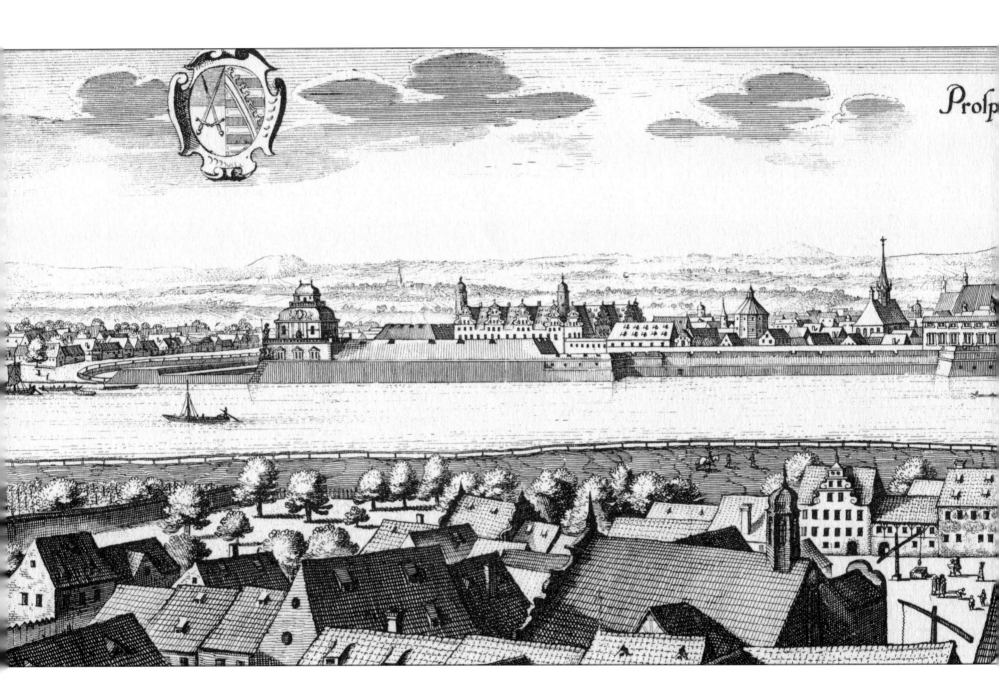

Prosp

Der Brucken. Zu. Dresden.

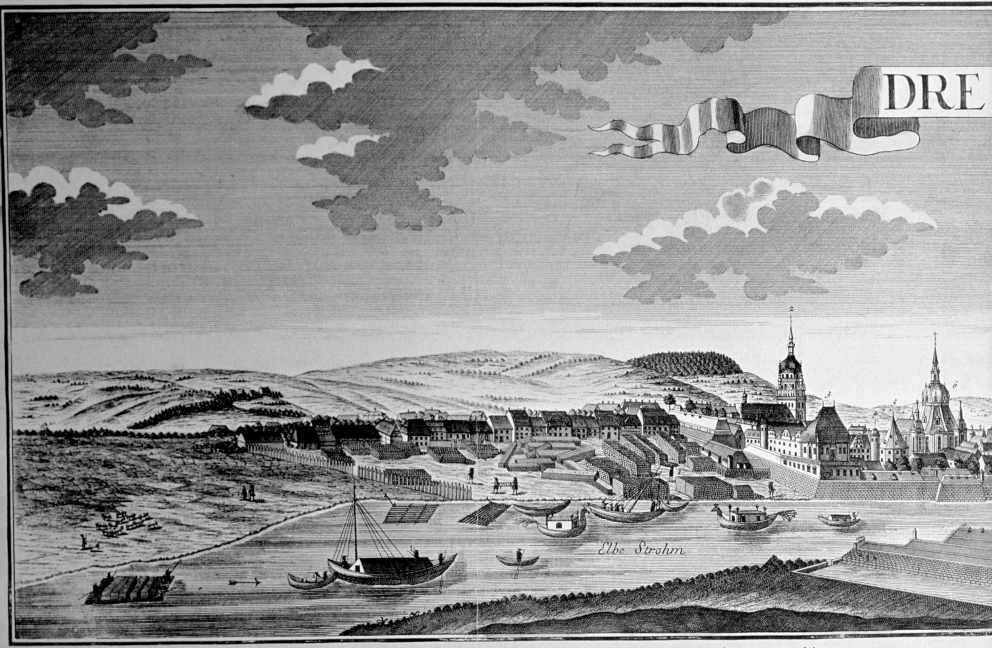

DRE

Elbe Strohm

1. Die Holtz lände.
2. Pfarr Kirch zum Heil. Creutz.
3. Lust Hauß sonst die Iungfer genant.

4. Daß Zeug Hauß
5. Pulver Thurn.
6. Neue Frauen Kirch.

7. Alt-Dresnische Thor.
8. Daß Schloß.
9. Opern Hauß.

Cum Priv. Sac. Cæs. May.

DEN.

Alt Dresden

0. Zwinger Garten.
1. Iäger Hoff.
2. Rath-Hauß in Alt Dresden.

13. Daß Block-Hauß auf der Brucken.
14. Cadets Hauß.
15. Proviant Häußer

16. Daß Schwartze Thor.

Herol Ir Wolffü excud Aug V

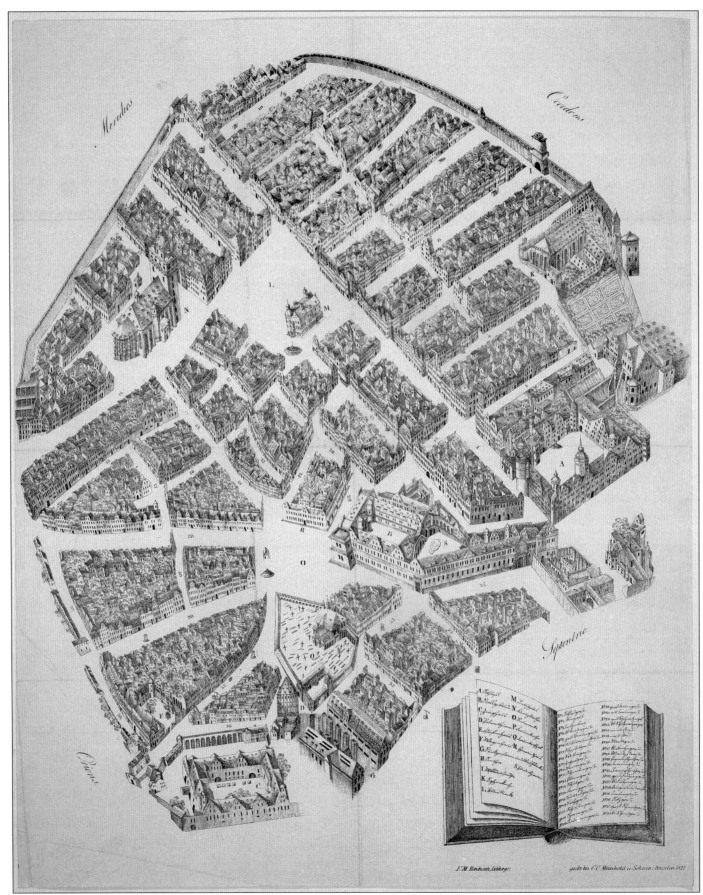

Meridies

Occidens

Septentrio

Oriens

F.M. Reibisch, lithogr.

gedr. bei C.C. Meinhold u. Söhnen Dresden 1827

PLAN DE LA VILLE ET RESIDENCE DE DRESDE.

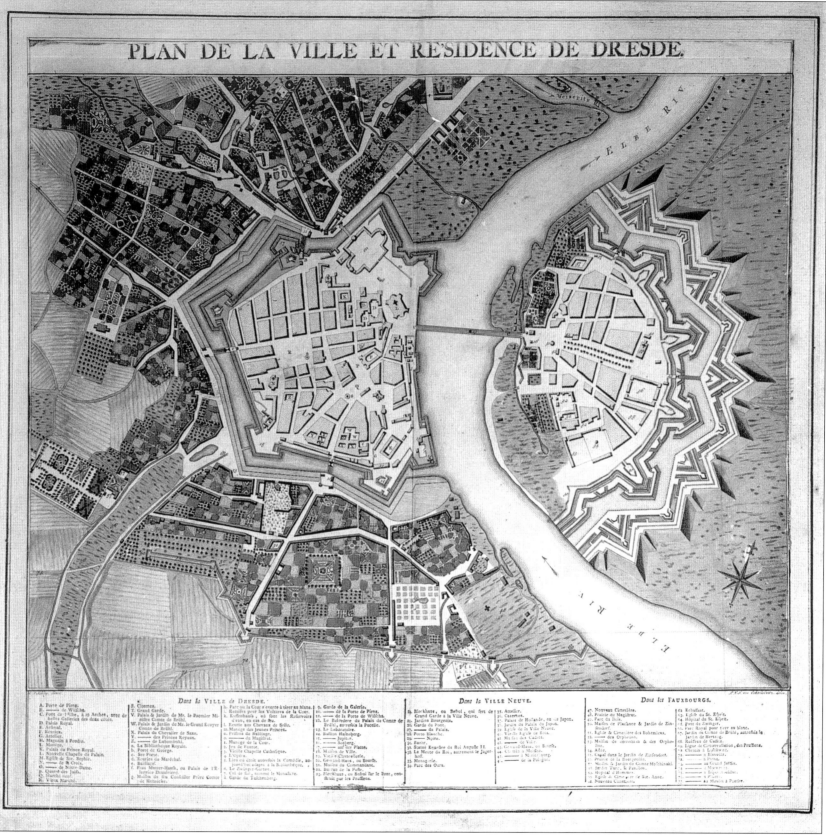

1750

PORTRÄT EINER BAROCKEN STADT

Bellottos fast fotorealistische Stadtansichten basieren auf genauer Beobachtung und der Verwendung der Camera Obscura. Die im Barock planmäßig ausgebaute Stadt bot eine Vielzahl lohnender Motive, die auch heute nichts von ihrer Lebendigkeit eingebüßt haben.

∾ ∾ ∾

PORTRAIT OF A CITY

Bellottos large scale panoramas are almost photorealistic. They are based on exact observations and the use of a camera obscura. Urban development was well structured in the Baroque period and thus provided a treasure trove of vistas for artists. The works are as engaging as they were at the time they were painted.

CONCERTOS FOR THE DRESDEN ORCHESTRA

Antonio Vivaldi (1678-1741)
CONCERTO "PER L'ORCHESTRA DI DRESDA" IN
G MINOR FOR TWO SOLO VIOLINS, TWO RECORDERS,
TWO OBOES, BASSOON, STRINGS AND B. C., RV 577

[1]   1. (without tempo designation) 3:40
[2]   2. Largo non molto 1:43
[3]   3. Allegro 3:23

Roland Straumer, violin I
Michael Frenzel, violin II
Eckart Haupt, recorder I
Gudrun Jahn, recorder II
Andreas Lorenz, oboe I
Wolfgang Klier, oboe II
Günter Klier, bassoon I
Bernd Rose, bassoon II
Michael-Christfried Winkler, continuo harpsichord

Georg Philipp Telemann (1681-1767)
CONCERTO IN D MAJOR FOR VIOLINO CONCERTATO,
CORNO DA CACCIA, CELLO OBLIGATO, BASSOON, THREE
VIOLINS, (THREE OBOES), TWO VIOLAS AND B.C.
(DRESDEN VERSION FROM JOHANN GEORG PISENDEL,
2ND MOVEMENT ARRANGED BY LUDWIG GÜTTLER)

[4]   1. Vivace 3:47
[5]   2. Adagio 3:39
[6]   3. Allegro 4:26

Roland Straumer, violin
Ludwig Güttler, corno da caccia
Joachim Bischof, violoncello
Hans-Peter Steger, bassoon

Johann David Heinichen (1683-1729)
CONCERTO IN F MAJOR FOR TWO TRANSVERSE FLUTES,
TWO OBOES, TWO BASSOONS, SOLO VIOLIN, TWO
VIOLONCELLOS, STRINGS, (TWO OBOES), AND B.C.

[7]   1. Allegro 2:35
[8]   2. Andante 2:13
[9]   3. (without tempo designation) 2:23

Eckart Haupt, flute I
Ulrich Philipp, flute II
Andreas Lorenz, oboe I
Guido Titze, oboe II
Hans-Peter Steger, bassoon I
Bernd Rose, bassoon II
Roland Straumer, violin
Joachim Bischof, violoncello I
Günther Müller, violoncello II

Johann Friedrich Fasch (1688-1758)
CONCERTO IN D MAJOR FOR TWO TRUMPETS, TWO
HORNS, TWO OBOES, BASSOON, STRINGS AND B. C.

[10]   1. Allegro 3:27
[11]   2. Andante 2:17
[12]   3. Allegro 3:04

Ludwig Güttler, trumpet I
Mathias Schmutzler, trumpet II
Erich Markwart, horn I
Hartmut Schergaut, horn II
Andreas Lorenz, oboe
Guido Titze, oboe II
Hans-Peter Steger, bassoon

Johann Gottlieb Graun (1702/3-1771)
CONCERTO IN G MAJOR FOR TWO SOLO VIOLINS,
TWO HORNS, STRINGS, (TWO OBOES) AND B. C.

[13]   1. (without tempo designation) 5:46
[14]   2. Adagio 5:08
[15]   3. Allegro molto con spirito 6:11

Roland Straumer, violin I
Michael Frentzel, violin II
Mathias Schmutzler, corno da caccia I
Roland Rudolph, corno da caccia II

VIRTUOSI SAXONIAE · LUDWIG GÜTTLER

℗ 1993 edel records GmbH

Johann Joachim Quantz (1697-1773)
CONCERTO IN G MINOR FOR TWO FLUTES, STRINGS AND B. C.

[4]   1. Allegro 8:31
[5]   2. Amoroso 4:58
[6]   3. Presto 5:37

Eckart Haupt, flute I
Gudrun Jahn, flute II

Antonio Vivaldi (1678-1741)
CONCERTO IN D MAJOR FOR TWO VIOLINS, TWO
OBOES, BASSOON, STRINGS AND B. C., RV 564A

[7]   1. Allegro 4:31
[8]   2. Adagio non molto 2:12
[9]   3. Allegro 2:50

Roland Straumer, violin I
Michael Eckoldt, violin II
Andreas Lorenz, oboe I
Guido Titze, oboe II
Günter Klier, bassoon

Jan Dismas Zelenka (1679-1745)
CAPRICCIO IN A MAJOR FOR TWO OBOES, BASSOON,
TWO CORNI DA CACCIA, STRINGS AND B. C.

[10]   1. Allegro assai 5:47
[11]   2. Adagio 1:34
[12]   3. Aria 1. alternativamente.
        Allegro assai
        Aria 2. Andante 4:43
[13]   4. En tempo de canarie 2:28
[14]   5. Menuet 1.
        Menuet 2. 2:29
[15]   6. Andante 1:43
[16]   7. Paysan 1.
        Paysan 2. Canon in unisono 2:11

Andreas Lorenz, oboe I
Guido Titze, oboe II
Ludwig Güttler, corno da caccia I
Kurt Sandau, corno da caccia II
Günter Klier, bassoon

Basso continuo:
Joachim Bischof, violoncello (Telemann, Vivaldi, Zelenka)
Günter Müller, violoncello (Quantz)
Werner Zeibig, double-bass (Telemann, Vivaldi, Zelenka)
Friedrich Kircheis, harpsichord (Telemann, Vivaldi, Zelenka),
organ (Quantz)

VIRTUOSI SAXONIAE · LUDWIG GÜTTLER

℗ 1992 edel records GmbH

CONCERTOS FOR SEVERAL SOLO INSTRUMENTS

Georg Philipp Telemann (1681-1767)
CONCERTO IN D MAJOR FOR VIOLIN, THREE CORNI
DA CACCIA, TWO OBOES, STRINGS AND B. C.

[1]   1. Allegro 3:57
[2]   2. Grave 2:49
[3]   3. Presto 2:13

Roland Straumer, violin
Ludwig Güttler, corno da caccia I
Erich Markwart, corno da caccia II
Hartmut Schergaut, corno da caccia III

Concertos for the court of the Elector of Saxony

Antonio Vivaldi

Concerto in C major for two recorders, two theorbos, two mandolins, two "salmò", two violins "in tromba marina", cello, strings and b. c., RV 558

[1]   1. Allegro molto 5:27
[2]   2. Andante molto. Piano sempre 1:23
[3]   3. Allegro 2:55

Roland Straumer, violin
Heinz-Dieter Richter, violin
Eckart Haupt, recorder I
Gudrun Jahn, recorder II
Susanne Ehrhardt, salmò I
Lisa Klevit-Ziegler, salmò II
Wolfgang Katschner, mandolin I
Angelika Oertel, mandolin II
Hans Werner Apel, theorbo I
Lee Santana, theorbo II
Joachim Bischof, violoncello

Concerto in F major for oboe, strings and b. c., RV 455

[4]   1. (without tempo designation) 3:37
[5]   2. Grave 2:10
[6]   3. Allegro 2:48

Andreas Lorenz, oboe

Concerto in D minor for viola d'amore, lute, strings and b. c., RV 540

[7]   1. Allegro 6:12
[8]   2. Largo 3:42
[9]   3. Allegro 3:26

Wolfram Just, viola d'amore
Wolfgang Katschner, lute

Concerto in A major for violin, three violins "per eco in lontano", strings and b. c., RV 552

[10]   1. Allegro 6:39
[11]   2. Larghetto 3:56
[12]   3. Allegro 3:52

Roland Straumer, violin
Michael Frenzel, violin

Sinfonia in G major for strings and b. c., RV 149

[13]   1. Allegro molto 1:39
[14]   2. Andante 1:22
[15]   3. Allegro 1:58

Concerto in G minor for three oboes, bassoon, two recorders, violin, strings and b. c., RV 576

[16]   1. (Allegro) 4:31
[17]   2. Larghetto 2:39
[18]   3. Allegro 4:21

Roland Straumer, violin
Eckart Haupt, recorder
Ekkehard Hering, recorder
Andreas Lorenz, oboe
Günter Klier, bassoon

Basso continuo:
Friedrich Kircheis, harpsichord
Joachim Bischof, violoncello
Werner Zeibig, double-bass

Virtuosi Saxoniae · Ludwig Güttler

℗ 1993 edel records GmbH

Sacred music for the court of Saxony

Johann Adolf Hasse (1699-1783)

Mass in G minor (1783)

I. Kyrie
[1]   Kyrie eleison (chorus) 2:57
[2]   Christe eleison (soprano, altus) 4:32
[3]   Kyrie eleison (chorus) 1:54

II. Gloria
[4]   Gloria in excelsis Deo (chorus) 3:32
[5]   Gratias agimus tibi (chorus) 1:53
[6]   Domine Deus, Rex caelestis (bass) 2:22
[7]   Domine Fili unigenite (soprano) 4:09
[8]   Domine Deus (soprano, altus, tenor, bass) 2:41
[9]   Qui tollis peccata mundi (soprano, chorus) 7:57
[10]   Quoniam tu solus sanctus (chorus) 2:11
[11]   Cum Sancto Spiritu (chorus) 2:46

III. Credo
[12]   Credo in unum Deum (tenor, chorus) 2:25
[13]   Et incarnatus est (chorus) 1:04
[14]   Crucifixus etiam pro nobis (soprano, altus) 2:29
[15]   Et resurrexit tertia die (chorus) 3:00

IV. Motetto 5:28
[16]   Ad te levavi animam meam (soprano, altus)

V. Sanctus
[17]   Sanctus (chorus) 1:15
[18]   Benedictus (soprano) 3:36
[19]   Hosanna in excelsis (chorus) 1:03

VI. Agnus Dei
[20]   Agnus Dei (soprano, altus, chorus) 5:03

Dagmar Schellenberger, soprano
Axel Köhler, altus
Ralph Eschrig, tenor
Egbert Junghanns, bass

Friedrich Kircheis, organ
Andreas Lorenz, oboe [9]
Hans-Peter Steger, bassoon

Thüringischer Akademischer Singkreis
Chorus Master: Wolfgang Unger

Virtuosi Saxoniae · Ludwig Güttler

℗ 1992 edel records GmbH

b. c. = basso continuo

Pieter van der Aa
ANSICHT DER STADT DRESDEN
(VIEW OF DRESDEN)
1729, Kupferstich (etching)
Galerie Agreable du Monde
p. 6
Johann Alexander Thiele
BLICK VON DEN LÖSNITZHÖHEN
AUF DRESDEN
(VIEW TO DRESDEN FROM
THE LÖSNITZHÖHEN)
Detail, 1751, 103 x 156 cm
p. 6/7

Johann Alexander Thiele
BLICK VON DEN LÖSNITZHÖHEN
AUF DRESDEN
(VIEW TO DRESDEN FROM
THE LÖSNITZHÖHEN)
1751, 103 x 156 cm
p. 8/9

Johann Alexander Thiele
WEG NACH BAUTZEN
(THE ROAD TO BAUTZEN)
BLICK AUF DRESDEN AUS DER
GEGEND VON COSSEBAUDE
(VIEW OF DRESDEN FROM THE
REGION OF COSSEBAUDE)
Detail, ca. 1745
Schwerin, Staatliches Museum
p. 10/11

Johann Alexander Thiele
WEG NACH BAUTZEN
(THE ROAD TO BAUTZEN)
BLICK AUF DRESDEN AUS DER
GEGEND VON COSSEBAUDE
(VIEW OF DRESDEN FROM THE
REGION OF COSSEBAUDE)
ca. 1745, Schwerin, Staatliches Museum
p. 12/13

Johann Alexander Thiele
ELBEBRÜCKE IN NEUSTADT –
ANSICHT VON DRESDEN MIT
DER AUGUSTUSBRUECKE
(VIEW OF DRESDEN WITH
THE AUGUSTUS BRIDGE)
1745, 104 x 153 cm
p. 14/15

Bernardo Bellotto, gen. Canaletto
DRESDEN VOM LINKEN ELBUFER
UNTERHALB DER FESTUNGSWERKE
(DRESDEN FROM THE LEFT BANK OF
THE ELBE, BELOW THE OLD CITY WALL)
Detail, 1748, 135 x 238 cm
p. 16/17

Bernardo Bellotto, gen. Canaletto
DRESDEN VOM LINKEN ELBUFER
UNTERHALB DER FESTUNGSWERKE
(DRESDEN FROM THE LEFT BANK OF
THE ELBE, BELOW THE OLD CITY WALL)
Detail, 1748, 135 x 238 cm
p. 18/19

Bernardo Bellotto, gen. Canaletto
DRESDEN VOM LINKEN ELBUFER
UNTERHALB DER FESTUNGSWERKE
(DRESDEN FROM THE LEFT BANK OF
THE ELBE, BELOW THE OLD CITY WALL)
1748, 135 x 238 cm
p. 20/21

Bernardo Bellotto, gen. Canaletto
DRESDEN VOM RECHTEN ELBUFER
UNTERHALB DER AUGUSTUSBRÜCKE
(VIEW OF DRESDEN FROM THE
RIGHT BANK OF THE ELBE BELOW
THE AUGUSTUS BRIDGE)
Detail, 1748, 133 x 237 cm
p. 22/23

Bernardo Bellotto, gen. Canaletto
DRESDEN VOM RECHTEN ELBUFER
UNTERHALB DER AUGUSTUSBRÜCKE
(VIEW OF DRESDEN FROM THE
RIGHT BANK OF THE ELBE BELOW
THE AUGUSTUS BRIDGE)
Detail, 1748, 133 x 237 cm
p. 24/25

Bernardo Bellotto, gen. Canaletto
DRESDEN VOM RECHTEN ELBUFER
UNTERHALB DER AUGUSTUSBRÜCKE
(VIEW OF DRESDEN FROM THE
RIGHT BANK OF THE ELBE BELOW
THE AUGUSTUS BRIDGE)
1748, 133 x 237 cm
p. 26/27

Bernardo Bellotto, gen. Canaletto
DRESDEN VOM LINKEN ELBUFER
OBERHALB DES ALTSTÄDTER
BRÜCKENKOPFES
(DRESDEN AS SEEN FROM THE LEFT
BANK OF THE ELBE ABOVE THE
ALTSTÄDTER BRIDGE HEAD)
Detail, 1748, 133 x 235 cm
p. 28/29

Bernardo Bellotto, gen. Canaletto
Dresden vom linken Elbufer
oberhalb des Altstädter
Brückenkopfes
(Dresden as seen from the left
bank of the Elbe, above the
Altstädter Bridge head)
1748, 133 x 235 cm
p. 30/31

Bernardo Bellotto, gen. Canaletto
Dresden vom rechten Elbufer
oberhalb der Augustusbrücke
(View of Dresden from the
right bank of the Elbe, above
the Augustus Bridge)
Detail, 1747, 132 x 236 cm
p. 32/33

Bernardo Bellotto, gen. Canaletto
Dresden vom rechten Elbufer
oberhalb der Augustusbrücke
(View of Dresden from the
right bank of the Elbe, above
the Augustus Bridge)
Detail, 1747, 132 x 236 cm
p. 34/35
Auf dieser Ansicht verewigte sich Bernardo
Bellotto (sitzend) selbst im Kreise der
Kollegen: Johann Alexander Thiele
deutet auf das Elbpanorama. Auch die
weiteren Personen im Vordergrund sind
identifizierbar. (In this scene Bernardo
Bellotto (seated) portrayed himself
surrounded by his peers: Johann Alexander
Thiele is shown pointing at the Elbe, others
in the foreground can be identified.)

Bernardo Bellotto, gen. Canaletto
Dresden vom rechten Elbufer
oberhalb der Augustusbrücke
(View of Dresden from the
right bank of the Elbe, above
the Augustus Bridge)
1747, 132 x 236 cm
p. 36/37

Ansicht der Stadt Dresden
aus dem Stammbuch des
Magisters Johannes Frentzel
(View of the City of Dresden
from the register of the
Magister, Johannes Frentzel)
ca. 1670, Deckfarbenmalerei (Gouache)
Leipzig, Universitaetsbibliothek
p. 38

Prospect der Bruecken zu Dresden
ca 1650, Kupferstich (etching) Wilhelm
Dilich, taken from: M. Zeiller, Topographia
Germaniae, Bd.12, Topographia Superioris
Saxoniae, Frankfurt, Matthaeus Merian)
p. 40/41

Ansicht von Dresden
(View of Dresden)
ca. 1735, kolorierter Kupferstich
(colorized copper engraving)
Dresden, Kupferstichkabinett
p. 42/43

Friedrich Martin Reibisch
Dresdener Altstadt im Jahr 1634
Dresden, Museum für Stadtgeschichte
p. 44
Plan de La Ville Et
Residence de Dresde
ca. 1755 nach dem Stich v. M. Seutter,
Dresden, Heimatkundliches
Schulmuseum – zerstört (after an
etching by v. M. Seutter, Dresden,
Heimatkundliches Schulmuseum – lost)
p. 45

Johann Samuel Mock
Bauern-Wirtschaft mit Kunst-
handlung und Theater am 25.6.1709
(«county fair» with art dealer
and theater on June 25th, 1709)
1709, Deckfarben (Gouache)
59 x 92 cm, Dresden, Kupferstich-Kabinett
p. 46/47

Johann Samuel Mock
Gesamtansicht von Palais und
Grossem Garten während der
Bauernwirtschaft am 25. Juni 1709
(Complete view of a palace
and large garden during the
«county fair» on June 25th, 1709)
1709, Deckfarben (Gouache)
59 x 91 cm, Dresden, Kupferstich-Kabinett
p. 48/49

Johann Alexander Thiele
Caroussel Comique
Aufzug im Zwinger
Karnevalsbelustigung unter
Koenig August dem Starken im Hof
des Zwinger am 17. Februar 1722
(Carnival amusements during the
reign of King August «the strong»
in the courtyard of the Zwinger
on the 17th of February, 1722)
before 1725, 106 x 168 cm
Gegenstück zu p. 56/57
(counterpiece to page 56/57)
p. 50/51

Johann Alexander Thiele
Caroussel Comique
Aufzug im Zwinger
Karnevalsbelustigung unter
Koenig August dem Starken im Hof
des Zwinger am 17. Februar 1722
(Carnival amusements during the
reign of King August „the strong"
in the courtyard of the Zwinger
on the 17th of February, 1722)
Detail, before 1725, 106 x 168 cm
Gegenstück zu p. 52/53
(counterpiece to page 52/53)
p. 52/53

Johann Alexander Thiele
CAROUSSEL COMIQUE
AUFZUG IM ZWINGER
KARNEVALSBELUSTIGUNG UNTER
KOENIG AUGUST DEM STARKEN IM HOF
DES ZWINGER AM 17. FEBRUAR 1722
(CARNIVAL AMUSEMENTS DURING THE
REIGN OF KING AUGUST «THE STRONG»
IN THE COURTYARD OF THE ZWINGER
ON THE 17TH OF FEBRUARY, 1722)
before 1725, 106 x 168 cm
Gegenstück zu p. 52/53)
(counterpiece to page 52/53)
p. 54/55

Johann Alexander Thiele
CAROUSSEL COMIQUE
AUFZUG IM ZWINGER
KARNEVALSBELUSTIGUNG UNTER
KOENIG AUGUST DEM STARKEN IM HOF
DES ZWINGER AM 17. FEBRUAR 1722
(CARNIVAL AMUSEMENTS DURING THE
REIGN OF KING AUGUST «THE STRONG»
IN THE COURTYARD OF THE ZWINGER
ON THE 17TH OF FEBRUARY, 1722)
Detail, before 1725, 106 x 168 cm
Gegenstück zu p. 52/53
(counterpiece to page 52/53)
p. 56/57

Johann Samuel Mock
FUSSTURNIER AUF DEM
DRESDNER ALTMARKT
(FOOT TOURNAMENT ON
DRESDEN'S ALTMARKT)
1735, Gouache, Dresden, Kupferstichkabinett
p. 58/59

Bernardo Bellotto, gen. Canaletto
DER ALTMARKT IN DRESDEN
VON DER SCHLOSSGASSE AUS
(ALTMARKT AS SEEN FROM
SCHLOSSGASSE)
Detail, 1751, 137 x 238 cm
p. 60/61

Bernardo Bellotto, gen. Canaletto
DER ALTMARKT IN DRESDEN
VON DER SCHLOSSGASSE AUS
(ALTMARKT AS SEEN FROM
SCHLOSSGASSE)
1751, 137 x 238 cm
p. 62/63

Bernardo Bellotto, gen. Canaletto
DER ALTMARKT IN DRESDEN
VON DER SEEGASSE AUS
(ALTMARKT AS SEEN FROM SEEGASSE)
Detail, 1751, 137 x 239 cm
p. 64/65

Bernardo Bellotto, gen. Canaletto
DER ALTMARKT IN DRESDEN
VON DER SEEGASSE AUS
(ALTMARKT AS SEEN FROM SEEGASSE)
Detail, 1751, 137 x 239 cm
p. 66/67

Bernardo Bellotto, gen. Canaletto
DER ALTMARKT IN DRESDEN
VON DER SEEGASSE AUS
(ALTMARKT AS SEEN FROM SEEGASSE)
Detail, 1751, 137 x 239 cm
p. 68/69

Bernardo Bellotto, gen. Canaletto
DER NEUMARKT IN DRESDEN
VON DER MORITZSTRASSE AUS
(NEUMARKT IN DRESDEN AS
SEEN FROM MORITZSTRASSE)
Detail, 1749–1751, 135 x 237 cm
p. 70/71

Bernardo Bellotto, gen. Canaletto
DER NEUMARKT IN DRESDEN
VOM JÜDENHOFE AUS
(NEUMARKT IN DRESDEN AS
SEEN FROM THE JÜDENHOFE)
Detail, 1749–1751, 136 x 237 cm
p. 72/73

Bernardo Bellotto, gen. Canaletto
DER NEUMARKT IN DRESDEN
VOM JÜDENHOFE AUS
(NEUMARKT IN DRESDEN AS
SEEN FROM THE JÜDENHOFE)
Detail, 1749–1751, 136 x 237 cm
p. 74/75

Bernardo Bellotto, gen. Canaletto
DER NEUMARKT IN DRESDEN
VOM JÜDENHOFE AUS
(NEUMARKT IN DRESDEN AS
SEEN FROM THE JÜDENHOFE)
1749–1751, 136 x 237 cm
p. 76/77

Sofern nicht anders angegeben handelt es sich um mit Öl auf Leinwand ausgeführte Werke mit Standort Dresden, Gemäldegalerie alter Meister.
If not otherwise specified, all works of art are rendered in oil on canvas—collection Old Masters Picture Gallery, Dresden, Germany.

Bernardo Bellotto, gen. Canaletto
DIE FRAUENKIRCHE IN DRESDEN
(FRAUENKIRCHE IN DRESDEN)
Detail, 1751–1753, 193 x 186 cm
p. 78/79

Bernardo Bellotto, gen. Canaletto
DIE FRAUENKIRCHE IN DRESDEN
(FRAUENKIRCHE IN DRESDEN)
·
1751–1753, 193 x 186 cm
p. 80
DIE EHEMALIGE KREUZKIRCHE
IN DRESDEN
(THE FORMER KREUZKIRCHE
IN DRESDEN)
1751–1753, 196 x 186 cm
p. 81

Bernardo Bellotto, gen. Canaletto
DIE TRÜMMER DER EHEMALIGEN
KREUZKIRCHE IN DRESDEN
(THE RUINS OF THE FORMER
KREUZKIRCHE IN DRESDEN)
1765, 80 x 110 cm
p. 82/83

1760 war die Kreuzkirche nach preußischem
Beschuss zerstört, der Turm aber
stehengeblieben. Nach heftigen Regengüssen
stürzte er ein und musste abgetragen werden.
(The Kreuzkirche was destroyed by
Prussian fire in 1760, but the tower remained
standing. Heavy rains caused it to collapse
and necessitated removal of the rubble.)

Bernardo Bellotto, gen. Canaletto
DER NEUSTÄDTERMARKT IN DRESDEN
(NEUSTÄDTERMARKT IN DRESDEN)
Detail, 1750/51, 134 x 236 cm
p. 84/85

Bernardo Bellotto, gen. Canaletto
DER NEUSTÄDTERMARKT IN DRESDEN
(NEUSTÄDTERMARKT IN DRESDEN)
1750/51, 134 x 236 cm
p. 86/87

Bernardo Bellotto, gen. Canaletto
DER ZWINGERHOF IN DRESDEN
(ZWINGERHOF IN DRESDEN)
Detail, 1749–1753, 132 x 236 cm
p. 88/89

Bernardo Bellotto, gen. Canaletto
DER ZWINGERHOF IN DRESDEN
(ZWINGERHOF IN DRESDEN)
1749–1753, 132 x 236 cm
p. 90/91

Bernardo Bellotto, gen. Canaletto
DER ZWINGERGRABEN IN DRESDEN
(ZWINGERGRABEN IN DRESDEN)
Detail, 1749–1753, 133 x 235 cm
p. 92/93

Bernardo Bellotto, gen. Canaletto
DER ZWINGERGRABEN IN DRESDEN
(ZWINGERGRABEN IN DRESDEN)
1749–1753, 133 x 235 cm
p. 94/95

Bernardo Bellotto, gen. Canaletto
DIE EHEMALIGEN
FESTUNGSWERKE IN DRESDEN
(THE OLD FORTIFICATION
WALLS IN DRESDEN)
Detail, 1748–1751, 132 x 236 cm
p. 96/97

Bernardo Bellotto, gen. Canaletto
DIE EHEMALIGEN
FESTUNGSWERKE IN DRESDEN
(THE OLD FORTIFICATION
WALLS IN DRESDEN)
1748–1751, 132 x 236 cm
p. 98/99

Johann Christian Clausen Dahl
BLICK AUF DRESDEN IM MONDSCHEIN
(VIEW OF DRESDEN IN
THE MOONLIGHT)
1839, Dresden
Museum für Geschichte der Stadt Dresden
p. 100/101